*This journal is dedicated to my
inspiration in living a life of ease:*

*My children,
grandchildren
&
husband*

ISBN 978-0-692-18805-7

The ABC's from Chaos to Ease "A Journal to Cultivate Calm"
Written by: LeAnn Elkins
Design & Layout by: Karen Theusen | karentheusen@gmail.com

Simple Intentions: Tools for Transformation
www.simpleintentions.com

Printed by CreateSpace, An Amazon.com Company

Name:

"I am at a place in my life
where ease is my priority
and chaos cannot exist."

What If...

What if you could truly describe your life as being content, calm, happy and joyful while filled with energy, connection, freedom, and creativity? It is absolutely possible to live in ease amid the chaos -- both internally, how you feel; and externally, how you respond. While you may not call your own life chaotic or even stressful, we live in a world where there is chaos all around. It is how we choose to react and "be" in the chaos around us that will allow us to live in ease.

This doesn't mean that life is always easy. In fact it is downright messy, sad and hard at times. However, through having strategies and practiced daily behaviors that support and guide us, we can get through even the tough times with courage and grace.

The ABC's from Chaos to Ease is a journal suggesting twenty-six ways of "being" (with a couple of "doing's" thrown in) to support this way of life. While the suggestions and thought provoking questions presented aren't the only ways of cultivating ease, may they serve as a catalyst to define and create what will work in your own life. Whether you are navigating the teen years (or parenting a teen), attending university, starting off in your professional life, raising young children, taking care of family, or transitioning to something new personally or professionally, there is a way to cultivate a life of calm.

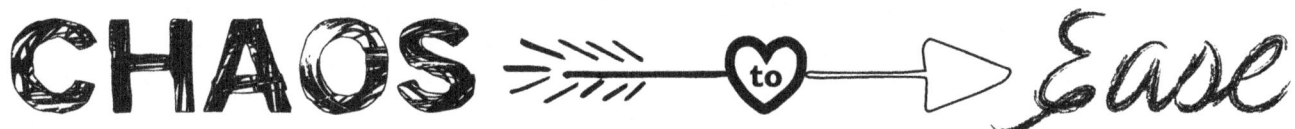

2

How to Use Journal

There are four pages for each letter of the alphabet. The first page shares the behavior, or way of being, with a short description. The second page has questions to reflect upon and answer. The third and fourth pages are supporting quotes or information and space to write your reflections.

While there is no single way to work through the journal, here are some ideas:

1. Complete the journal in just a few sittings.

2. Start with the letter A and work though one letter a day for 26 days.

3. Open the journal to a random page and reflect/respond.

4. Take one letter a week for 26 weeks.

5. Work through it together with a partner, family member(s) or friend.

My intention for your time spent in this journal is that you fill each page noticing where you are on your journey, answering questions, coloring, doodling and reflecting to cultivate your own calm.

Let's start with some simple definitions of
CHAOS & *Ease*

CHAOS:

Disorder & confusion

Absence of difficulty

Where is there **CHAOS** & stress in my life?*

*Don't take this lightly, and be honest with yourself. The list may
 contain friends or loved ones–it's okay!

6

Where is there *Ease* in my life?

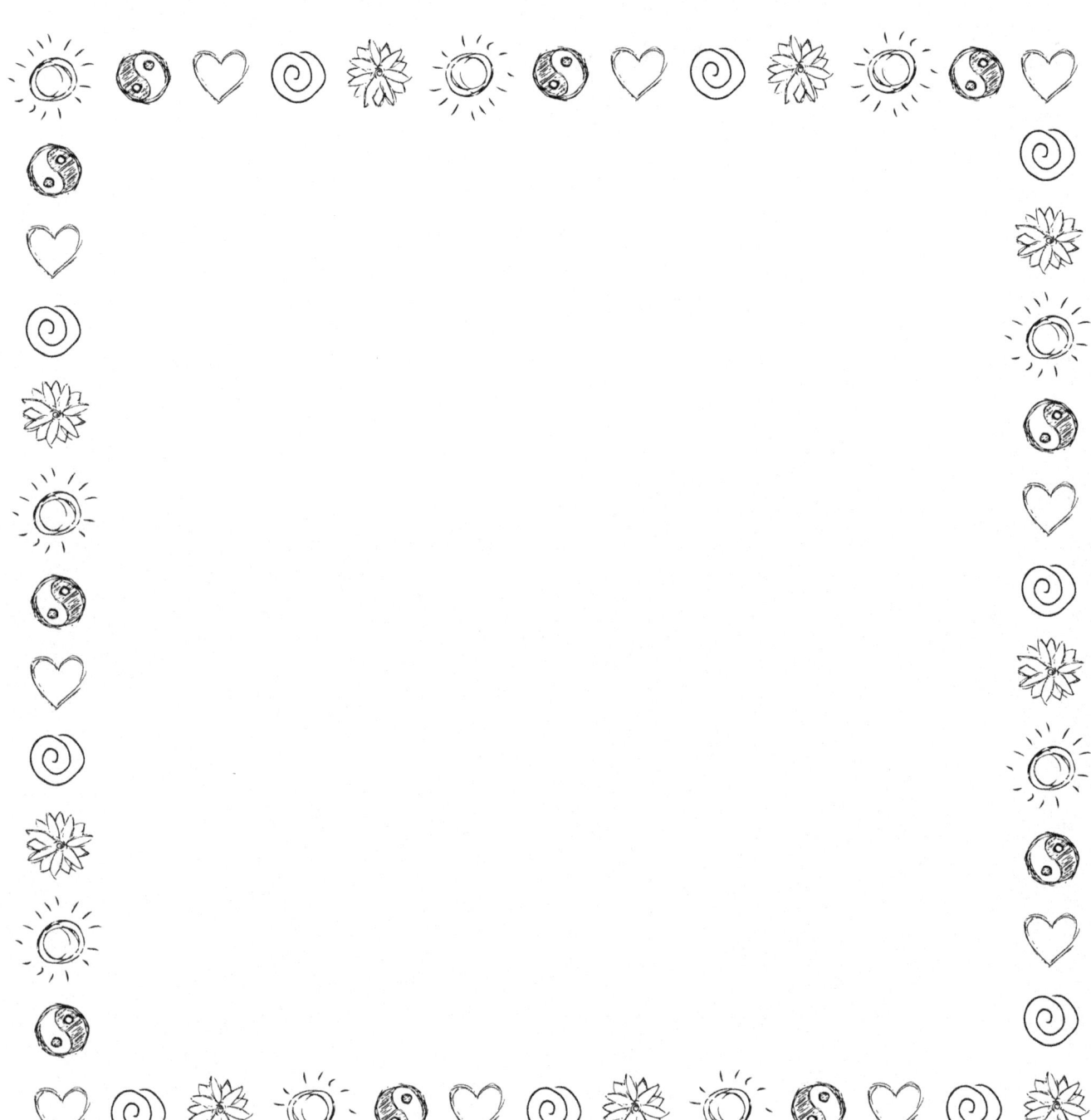

A to Z

A is for ___Attitude___

B is for ___Breathe___

C is for ___Clutter Be Gone___

D is for ___Drama - Free___

E is for ___Easy - Going___

F is for ___Free - Time___

G is for ___Gratitude___

H is for ___Happiness___

I is for ___Intuition___

J is for ___Joy___

K is for ___Kindness___

L is for ___Love - All of You___

M is for ___Meditation___

N is for ___Nourish___

O is for ___Optimistic___

P is for ___Patience___

Q is for ___Quality___

R is for ___Rituals___

S is for ___Self - Care___

T is for ___Truth___

U is for ___U Are Enough___

V is for ___Visualize___

W is for ___Withhold Judgement___

X is for ___eXecute___

Y is for ___Yin Yoga___

Z is for ___Zen___

9

A is for *Attitude*

To experience ease one must first start with an openness to approach life in a positive way. Coming from a place of optimism in our thoughts, feelings, and actions will attract positive life experiences. With health benefits such as increased life span, lower rates of depression, better heart health and coping skills during stressful times - why not start with a positive attitude?

Notes about *Attitude:*

_____

_____

_____

_____

_____

A

Attitude

 *Write down words that describe having a positive attitude.*

 *How are you approaching life with a positive attitude?*

_____

_____

_____

_____

_____

A
Attitude

Mindful Attitudes

- Accepting
- Beginner's mind -"openness"
- Generous
- Let it go!
- Patient
- Positive
- Trusting
- Withhold judgement

A
Attitude

_____

_____

_____

_____

_____

_____

_____

_____

_____

_____

A
Attitude

B is for Breathe

Deep breathing can quickly reduce our stress - whatever that may be and however it may be showing up. By really focusing on our breath - the inhale followed by the deep exhale, we turn our focus entirely inward. This simple action lowers our heart rate, calms the mind, increases the intake of oxygen to help nourish the body and brain and calms anxiety (to name a few of the benefits).

Notes about *Breathe*:

_____

_____

_____

_____

_____

B
Breathe

 *In what situations would it be helpful to slow down and focus on your breath?*

Inhale

Try It!

Exhale
(and repeat)

 *Journal your experience.*

_____

_____

_____

_____

B
Breathe

_____

_____

_____

_____

_____

_____

_____

_____

_____

_____

B
Breathe

C is for Clutter, be gone!

Clutter, whether it be external or internal, is another way to describe chaos. External clutter may be material "things," a messy room, social/personal obligations, television shows we watch, books we read, time on social media or perhaps even people in our lives. Internal clutter is those endless thoughts and voices that keep us up at night, make us second guess decisions and tell us "we are not enough!" Identifying the clutter and recognizing the impact it is having on us will help move us from chaos to ease.

Notes about *Clutter, be gone!*

_____

_____

_____

_____

C
Clutter, be gone!

List external
clutter in your life:

List internal
clutter in your life:

_____

_____

_____

_____

_____

C
Clutter, be gone!

When we throw out the physical clutter, we clear out our minds. When we throw out the mental clutter, we clear our souls.
-Gail Blanke

Have nothing in your house that you do not know to be useful, or believe to be beautiful.
-Williams Morris

Don't be a Victim of Negative
-Self Talk-
Remember
You are Listening.

Clutter is not just physical stuff. It's old ideas, toxic relationships and bad habits. Clutter is anything that does not support your better self.
-Eleanor Brown

Don't believe everything you think.

What I know for sure is that when you declutter-whether it's on your home, your head, or your heart-it is astounding what will flow into that space that will enrich you, your life, and your family.
-Peter Walsh

A place for everything, and everything in its place.
-Mrs. Beeton

Clutter, be gone!

_____

_____

_____

_____

_____

_____

_____

_____

_____

_____

_____

ℂ
Clutter, be gone!

D is for Drama - Free

Drama - also known as a constant need for Chaos - is an addictive behavior that can lead to anxiety and stress. It shows up in our lives through one crisis after another. Drama is often a distraction to staying present. Whether you have a lot of drama personally, have friends with continual drama (we all have these people in our lives) or allow the drama of the world around you to penetrate through you, now is the time to commit to a drama - free zone!

Notes about *Drama - Free:*

_____

_____

_____

_____

D
Drama - Free

 *In what ways does drama show up in your own life?*

 *How will you create a drama - free zone?*

_____

_____

_____

_____

_____

D
Drama - Free

Drama

does not just show up at your door.

Either you

Create it , invite it,

or associate with it.

D
Drama - Free

_____

_____

_____

_____

_____

_____

_____

_____

_____

_____

_____

𝔻
Drama - Free

E is for Easy - Going

Through an easy-going way of living, we approach situations in a relaxed and understanding manner. Being easy-going is about staying calm, positive, patient and even-tempered and supports our desire to be in EASE! On the other hand, if we are uptight, negative, anxious and judgmental we will feed the chaos and stress.

Notes about *Easy - Going:*

_____

_____

_____

_____

E
Easy - Going

Describe easy - going behavior.

What recent situation would have benefitted from a more relaxed approach?

_____

_____

_____

_____

_____

E
Easy - Going

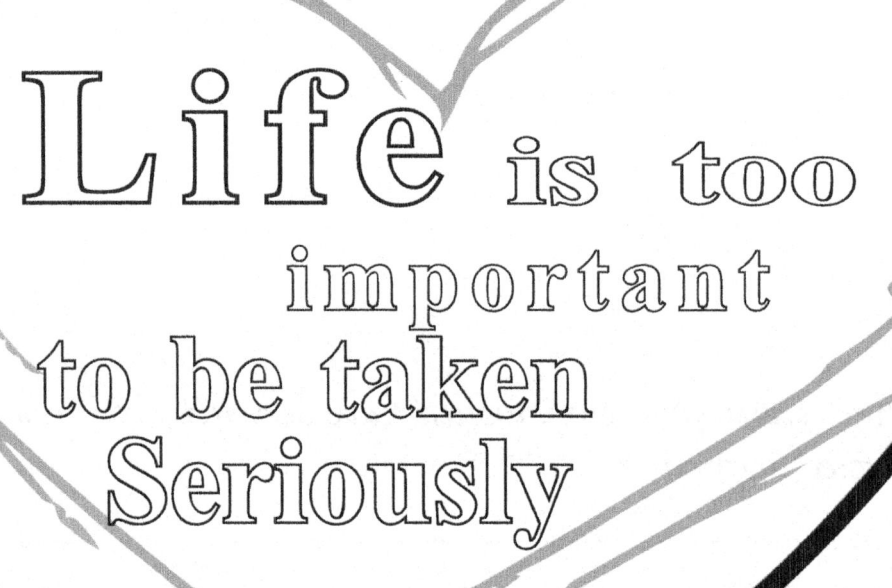

Life is too important to be taken Seriously

oscar wilde

E
Easy - Going

28

_____

_____

_____

_____

_____

_____

_____

_____

_____

_____

E
Easy - Going

 **F** is for *Free - Time*

We live in a world full of schedules and staying "busy" and may even pride ourselves on being busy. While schedules and other time management techniques may support us in feeling less chaotic, filling up all of our time leaves us no space. We lack space for creating, slowing down, spontaneity, resting or simply being! Merely taking a "time-out" or having a day without plans will improve vitality, decision making and performance.

Notes about *Free - Time:*

_____

_____

_____

_____

F
Free - Time

What does creating free - time/ space look like?

_____

_____

_____

_____

_____

M	T	W	Th	F	S	S

If you had more free - time / space, what benefits are you bound to receive:

   Physically _____

   _____

   _____

   Mentally _____

   _____

   _____

   Emotionally _____

   _____

   _____

F
Free - Time

THE TIME YOU ENJOY wasting Is NOT WASTED TIME.

bertrand russell

F
Free - Time

☯ ♡ ◎ ✾ ☼ *Reflections* ☯ ♡ ◎ ✾ ☼

F
Free - Time

G is for *Gratitude*

Being thankful and showing appreciation is often said to be the key to living a happy and fulfilled life. There is so much to be grateful for in our lives! In expressing an attitude of gratitude, we draw closer to friends, health, love, and bliss. As research shows, taking the time each day to be grateful improves physical and psychological health, enhances empathy, reduces aggression, makes us happier, and improves sleep.

Notes about *Gratitude:*

_____

_____

_____

_____

G
Gratitude

What are you grateful for today?

How could you practice having an attitude of gratitude?

_____

_____

_____

_____

_____

G
Gratitude

IF THE ONLY PRAYER
YOU EVER SAY IS
"THANK YOU"
THAT WILL
BE ENOUGH

eckhart tolle

GRACIAS

TAK!   todah!

MERCI   thanks

DANKE SCHOEN

Salamat

G
Gratitude

_____

_____

_____

_____

_____

_____

_____

_____

_____

_____

G
Gratitude

H is for *Happiness*

Being happy is more than putting a smile on our face and having a positive mood. Happiness is about living a life with meaning and purpose. It is a state of well-being and contentment. Happiness is about having practices that promote and support this well-being. In fact, scientific studies have been finding that happiness can make our hearts healthier, our immune systems stronger, and our lives longer.

Notes about *Happiness:*

_____

_____

_____

_____

Happiness

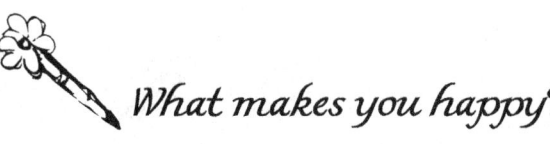 What makes you happy?

What practices will you do to promote your own well-being and happiness?

_____

_____

_____

_____

_____

H

Happiness

Because when you stop & look around, this life is pretty Amazing.

H
Happiness

Reflections

H

Happiness

I is for *Intuition*

Trust your intuition! You know, that sense of "knowing, without knowing". Those times when we just KNOW something is the right thing to do and BAM, WE'RE RIGHT (thank you intuition)! We also have those times when something just doesn't feel right–well, it probably isn't. PAY ATTENTION and TRUST YOUR GUT FEELINGS! No matter how good something looks, if it doesn't feel right, there is something wrong!

Notes about *Intuition:*

_____

_____

_____

_____

I

Intuition

Quiet your mind now and listen. What is your intuition telling you that you may not want to hear but need to hear?

_____

_____

_____

_____

_____

_____

_____

_____

I

Intuition

Steps to "LISTEN" to your *Intuition*

- ☼ Get still

- ☼ Listen

- ☼ Ask a question

- ☼ Journal whatever you hear

- ☼ Repeat Often

I
Intuition

_____

_____

_____

_____

_____

_____

_____

_____

_____

_____

_____

I
Intuition

J is for *Joy*

Delight + great pleasure + jubilation + triumph + glee + exuberance + elation + bliss = *Joy*. In choosing to live in joy, we not only experience a powerful state of being for ourselves, we pass it on to those around us. Joy is contagious! And like gratitude, the experience of joy has long-lasting positive effects.

Notes about *Joy:*

_____

_____

_____

_____

J

Joy

What does the expression "choose Joy" mean to you?

How would spreading joy improve your life and those around you?

_____

_____

_____

_____

_____

J

Joy

Joy

is what happens to
us when we allow
ourselves to
recognize how
good
things really are

marianne williamson

J
Joy

_____

_____

_____

_____

_____

_____

_____

_____

_____

_____

J
Joy

K is for *Kindness*

Being friendly, generous and considerate to self and others is living in kindness. We can choose to approach our daily interactions with the filter of being kind and it is through these acts of kindness that we do change the world moment by moment!

Notes about *Kindness:*

_____

_____

_____

_____

_____

K
Kindness

How do you show kindness and compassion to yourself and the people around you?

1 kind word can change someone's entire day. What are you willing to do everyday to spread kindness and hence change the world?

_____

_____

_____

_____

K
Kindness

BE KIND

WHENEVER POSSIBLE

It is Always

P - O - S - S - I - B - L - E

dali lama

K
Kindness

Reflections

K

Kindness

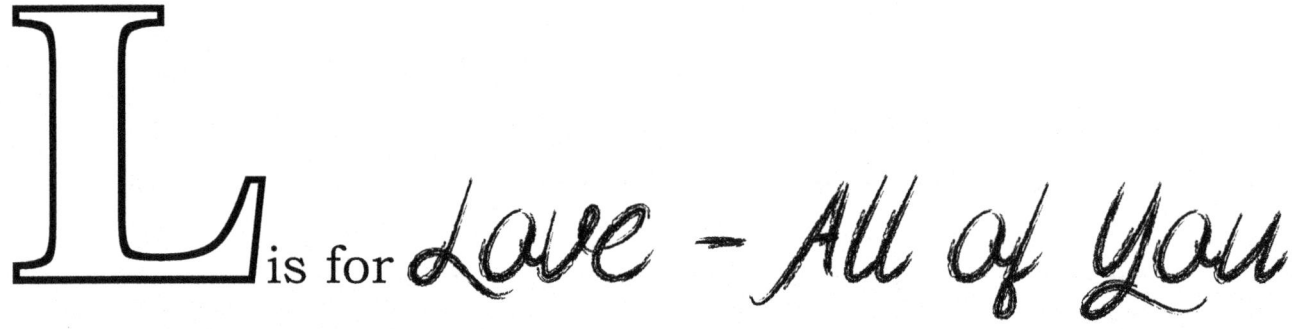

L is for *Love - All of You*

To love oneself–all of the parts of self–is the ultimate expression of self kindness and self acceptance. In honoring and showing a real concern for ALL aspects of our self, we find self compassion and love.

- sadness
- shame
- fear
- grief
- anger
- anxiety

- understanding
- courage
- hopefulness
- forgiveness
- joy
- love

Notes about *Love* - All of YOU:

_____

_____

_____

_____

L
Love - All of You

In thinking about self kindness/acceptance, what would you tell your:

 10 year old self:

 teenage self:

 young adult self:

 self today:

L
Love - All of You

Brainstorm below all of the things you love about yourself. Don't be shy!

L

Love - All of You

Reflections

L
Love – All of You

57

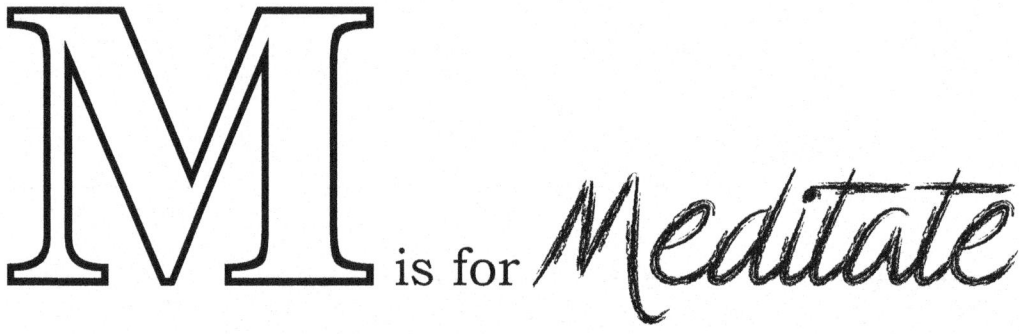
M is for *Meditate*

Meditation, at its core, is simply taking time (in silence) to think deeply and/or focus our minds. As a daily practice, we meditate to catch our breath, to prepare for a conversation, to slow down, to silence our minds and to let the wisdom within be heard. Meditation may be a quick minute or perhaps 20 or more. Some meditation styles with examples include: meditation in motion (walking & cooking), guided meditation (imagery & body scans), concentration meditation (mantras & breathing) or mindfulness meditation (awareness of thoughts & feelings). So many ways to meditate and I encourage you to give it a try!

Notes about *Meditate:*

_____

_____

_____

_____

M
Meditate

The quieter you become, the more you can hear.

ram dass

In considering the different meditation styles, check all that fit you and your style best.

☐   ☐   ☐   ☐

Motion   Guided   Concentration   Mindfulness

How will you fit a few moments of meditation time into your life?

_____

_____

_____

_____

_____

M
Meditate

Meditation

Step 1
Setting

Find quiet space that is free from distraction.

Step 2
Timer

Set timer to a gentle sound.

Step 3
Position

Sit as comfortably as possible.

Step 4
Close Eyes & Breathe

Gently close your eyes and breathe. Inhale slowly until lungs fill up then exhale smoothly and completely.

Step 5
Focus on Breath or Mantra

Repeat inhale and exhale paying attention to breath or repeating a mantra like "I am enough".

Step 6
Be Kind to Self

When your mind wanders, simply bring it back to breath or mantra.

Repeat until you hear timer

M
Meditate

Reflections

M
Meditate

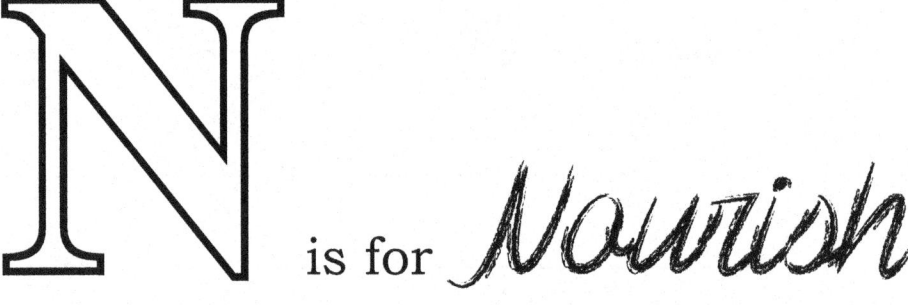

N is for *Nourish*

Providing nourishment to fuel a life of ease is made up of many aspects. Nourishment in what we choose to eat, to drink, and how we nourish our bodies with exercise and movement. Nourishment can also be the types of television shows or movies we watch, who we follow on social media and the books we read. Nourishment is a choice we make in the kinds of activities we participate in to refresh, revive and renew. Nourishment can also be the company we keep. Do they fuel you or diminish you?

Notes about *Nourish:*

_____

_____

_____

_____

_____

N

Nourish

What daily food, drink and exercise (movement) choices are you making to fuel your body with nourishment?

_____

_____

_____

_____

What are the different ways you provided other nourishment to yourself? From what you watched or read to what you did and who you spent time with.

_____

_____

_____

_____

N
Nourish

YOU GOTTA NOURISH

TO

FLOURISH

N
Nourish

64

_____

_____

_____

_____

_____

_____

_____

_____

_____

_____

_____

N
Nourish

O is for *Optimistic*

Why not be hopeful, positive and confident? When we approach our days with an optimistic perspective there are many benefits. We feel healthier, we *are* healthier, we don't sweat the small stuff, we have higher job satisfaction, *and* we are more resilient. Plus, optimism is contagious! Let's take the opportunity to spread the power of positivity by simply taking an optimistic stance!

Notes about *Optimistic:*

_____

_____

_____

_____

_____

O

Optimistic

 *I am Optimistic in these areas:*

 *I could be more Optimistic in these areas:*

Optimistic

Every Day
May Not Be
GOOD
but there is
Something Good
IN EVERY DAY.

Optimistic

_____

_____

_____

_____

_____

_____

_____

_____

_____

_____

Optimistic

 **P** is for *Patience*

Patience in self, others and situations, is not just simply waiting. Patience in terms of "ease" is in BEING HERE NOW! Staying in the moment, and not thinking about the future. This is harder than it sounds. Especially when it's used as a coping mechanism in those hard moments of life. You can be so busy looking ahead you miss the good parts of now!

Notes about *Patience:*

_____

_____

_____

_____

_____

P
Patience

Using the letters PATIENCE, describe your life right now.
(example: P=peaceful, A=action, T=tranquil)

P

A

T

I

E

N

C

E

P
Patience

Patience

is NOT
the ability to
wait but how you
ACT while you're
waiting.

joyce meyer

P
Patience

Reflections

P

Patience

Q is for Quality

Quality in terms of ease is about making discriminating choices around how we spend our time and with whom we spend it. Instead of focusing on quantity and doing a "bunch" of stuff, "checking-off" a big list of items, or having a large group of friends — we choose quality. Through this practice we can be present in our relationships and how we go about getting things done because we have carefully chosen how we fill our days.

Notes about *Quality*:

_____

_____

_____

_____

_____

Q
Quality

 *Your friends should support, motivate and inspire you. Which of your friends fits this criteria? Write their names in the cloud.*

 *Thinking about the next few days or weeks, what discriminating choices will you make to focus on Quality over Quantity?*

_____

_____

_____

_____

_____

Q
Quality

Don't count the things you do

DO THE THINGS

that count

Zig Ziglar

Quality

Reflections

Quality

R is for *Rituals*

Our morning ritual sets the tone of the day while our evening ritual is a way to celebrate and give thanks for the day. Through repetition of these rituals, they will become routine and something we look forward to each day. Our morning ritual may include a meditation, some stretching and a cup of tea! The evening ritual may be a bath, reading and journaling. The possibilities are endless! Intention at the start and end of each day will help strengthen the muscle of ease.

Notes about *Rituals*:

_____

_____

_____

_____

_____

ℝ
Rituals

List in the scroll above, all possible morning and evening rituals that fit your schedule and desires.

I will try these three morning and three evening rituals:

R
Rituals

Rituals

R

Rituals

R
Rituals

S is for *Self-Care*

While self-care for some may sound "selfish" it is essential to living a life of ease. Self-care is an active and powerful choice to engage mindfully in the activities and thoughts that are required to gain and/or maintain an optimal level of overall health and well-being! Through consistent self-care, we will improve our own self-compassion, feel better, and have more to give to others.

Notes about *Self-Care:*

_____

_____

_____

_____

_____

S
Self-Care

It is not selfish to do what is best for you.

mark sutton

What if you devoted time everyday to self care and loving yourself? What could you possibly create?

S
Self-Care

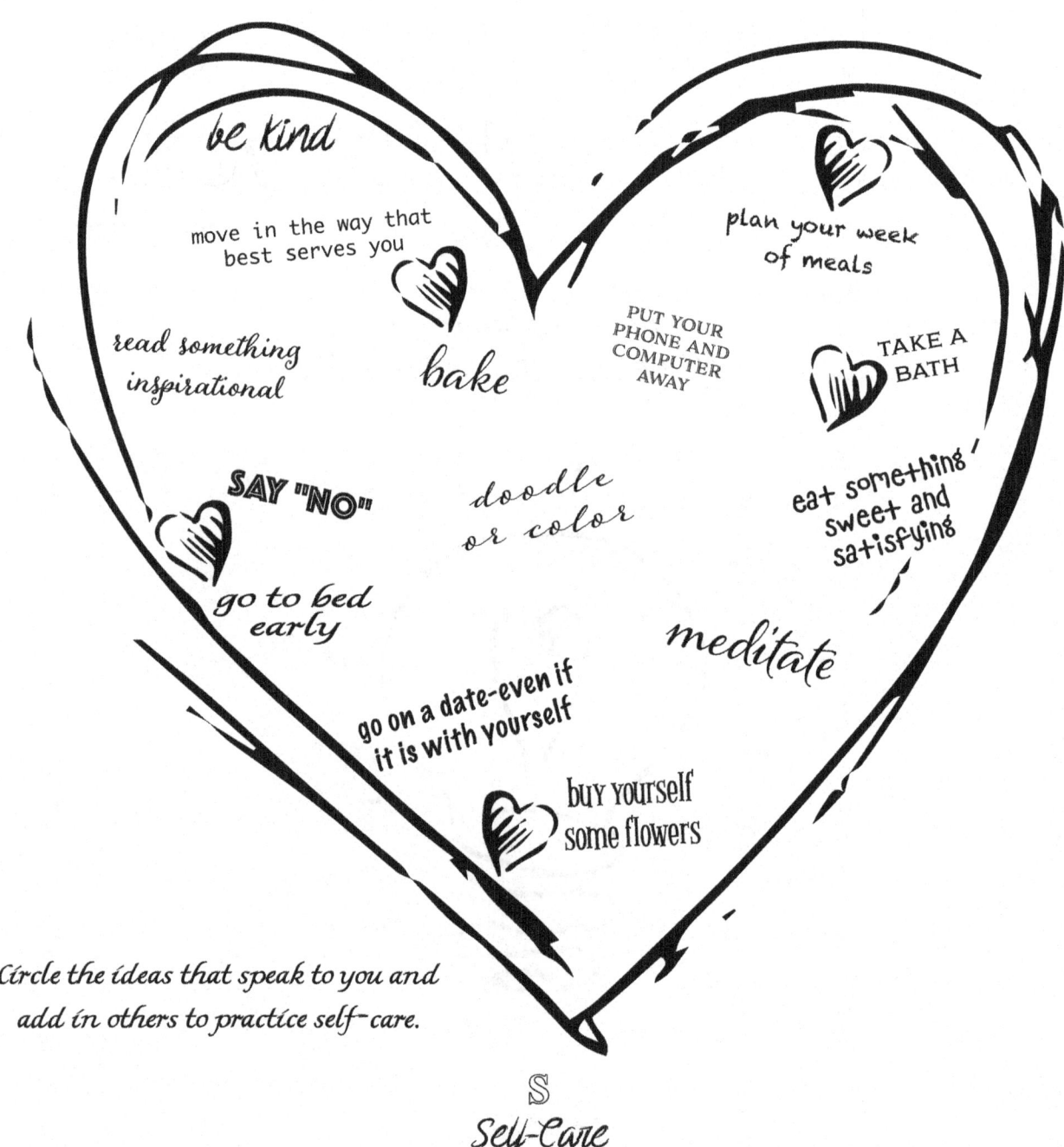

be kind

move in the way that best serves you

plan your week of meals

read something inspirational

bake

PUT YOUR PHONE AND COMPUTER AWAY

TAKE A BATH

SAY "NO"

doodle or color

eat something sweet and satisfying

go to bed early

meditate

go on a date-even if it is with yourself

buy yourself some flowers

Circle the ideas that speak to you and add in others to practice self-care.

S
Self-Care

_____

_____

_____

_____

_____

_____

_____

_____

_____

_____

S
Self-Care

T is for *Truth*

Truth–and being truthful–support a life of ease through reducing the stresses associated with living a lie. This means always being our own authentic selves. We demonstrate this truth through loving, honoring and respecting ourselves. When we are true to ourselves the unique and amazing individual that we are will awaken to realize our full potential.

Notes about *Truth:*

_____

_____

_____

_____

_____

T

Truth

 *How do you love, honor and respect yourself?*

 *How are you demonstrating authenticity and truth?*

 How do you know when you are not being true to yourself?

T
Truth

AUTHENTICITY

IS THE DAILY PRACTICE

of letting go of who we think we are

supposed to be and

embracing

who we are

brené brown

T
Truth

Reflections

T

Truth

U is for *U are Enough*

Yes, you are enough! Right here, right now, in this moment. You are lovable, beautiful and worthy. You don't need anyone's approval in order to be good enough. Say goodbye to the voice in your head saying you need to be thinner, smarter, fitter, wiser, prettier, wealthier...you are enough and you always were!

Notes about *U are Enough:*

_____

_____

_____

_____

_____

U

U are Enough

List what your inner voice says that makes you question your worth:

◎

◎

◎

◎

◎

Now cross all of those things out and write big and bold,

I am enough!

U
U are Enough

In case nobody told you today:

You are enough

You are enough

You are enough

You are enough

You are enough

U

U are Enough

92

_____

_____

_____

_____

_____

_____

_____

_____

_____

_____

U
U are Enough

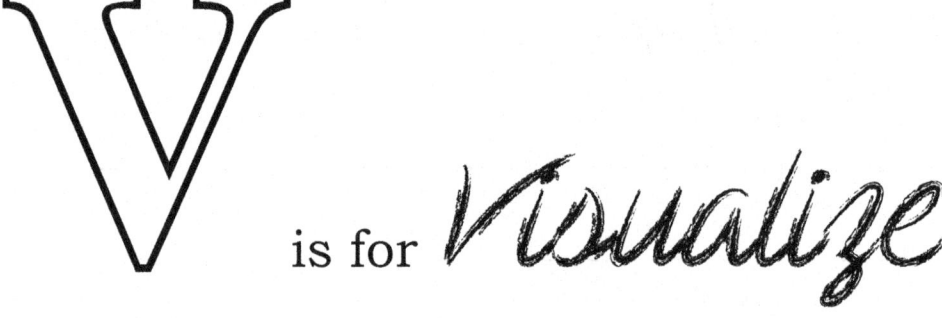
V is for *Visualize*

We have the ability to create what we visualize through stating and communicating the intention. Visualization requires us to not only want something, but to be able to see it and to believe in it. Through visualizing what ease looks like externally and feels like internally we will be supported in making choices that align with creating ease and calm in our lives.

Notes about *Visualize:*

_____

_____

_____

_____

_____

V

Visualize

Ease looks like:

Ease feels like:

V
Visualize

Everything you need -
your courage, strength,
compassion and love -
is already within you.

V
Visualize

_____

_____

_____

_____

_____

_____

_____

_____

_____

_____

_____

V

Visualize

W is for *Withhold Judgement*

What if we spent our days practicing empathy? This requires us to listen and withhold judgment. We often spend time judging self and others which causes us to be operating from a place of right/wrong and good/bad! Our thoughts are filled with shame, guilt, anger and fear! Let's live instead, by not judging, rather practicing being curious, empathetic, kind and caring.

Notes about *Withhold Judgement*

_____

_____

_____

_____

_____

W
Withhold Judgement

Take today or tomorrow and notice all of the times you either think or say out loud statements that are passing judgment. These may be about self or others, solo thoughts or thoughts shared/expressed with others. Write down your findings. _____

_____

_____

_____

Let's Practice

Spend a day living in empathy and withholding judgement about self and others. What did that look/feel like? How can that become your way of being? _____

_____

_____

_____

W

Withhold Judgement

Judging a  PERSON does not define who they are...

It defines WHO YOU ARE!

W
Withhold Judgement

_____

_____

_____

_____

_____

_____

_____

_____

_____

_____

_____

W
Withhold Judgement

X 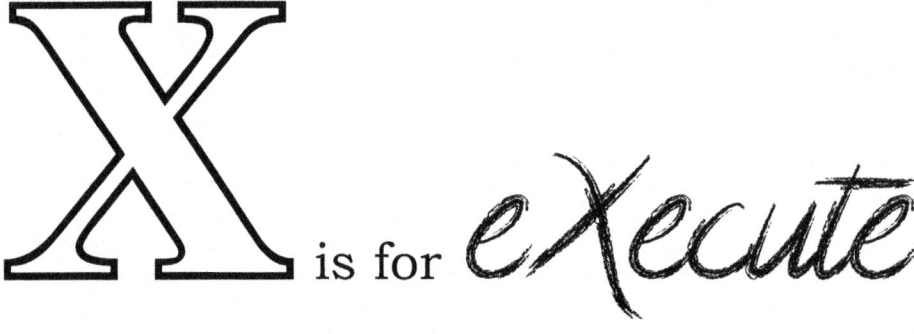 is for eXecute

This is one of the doings!" Living in ease does not mean NOT getting things done. But HOW we do things does matter. While we will have goals, objectives and targets - in work and in life - as we work on moving from Chaos to Ease, we change how we view and how we accomplish these targets. We can execute and stay in ease! All 26 letters will help us accomplish the goals.

Notes about eXecute:

_____

_____

_____

_____

_____

X
eXecute

After working through all of the other letters, what things have you already executed on to support living in ease?

♡

♡

♡

♡

♡

Review letters A to Z and all of your responses, what behaviors will you

Continue to do:

Start to do:

Stop doing:

to support living in ease?

X
eXecute

The journey of a thousand miles begins with one step

lao tzu

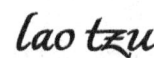

X
execute

_____

_____

_____

_____

_____

_____

_____

_____

_____

_____

_____

X
eXecute

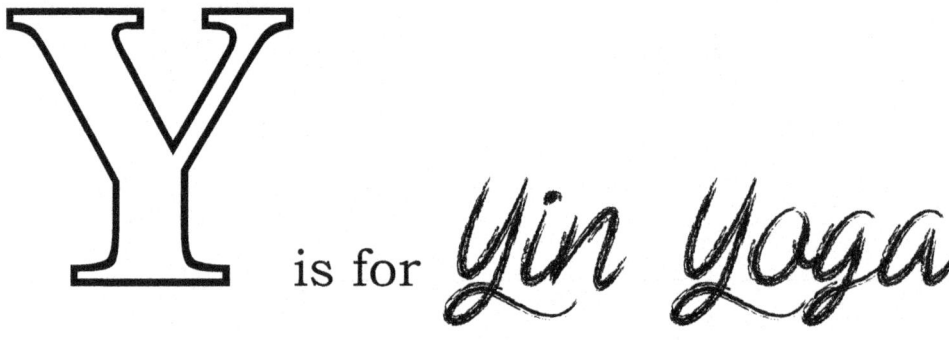

Y is for *Yin Yoga*

Finding enjoyable ways to move is key for each of us–from dancing to walking to playing with children (or whatever)! Just move! Another way may be Yin Yoga. Yin Yoga is for our overactive minds, our tired bodies and our busy days. It is a slow paced/passive style of yoga that involves poses being held for longer periods of time. Our bodies and minds will be grateful for this slower, yet energetic practice.

Notes about *Yin Yoga:*

_____

_____

_____

_____

_____

Y
Yin Yoga

Yin Yoga Supports:

- quieting your mind

- reducing stress and anxiety

- improving flexibility

- bringing stillness and calm

How will you find a way to give your body
and mind this gift?

_____

_____

_____

_____

Y
Yin Yoga

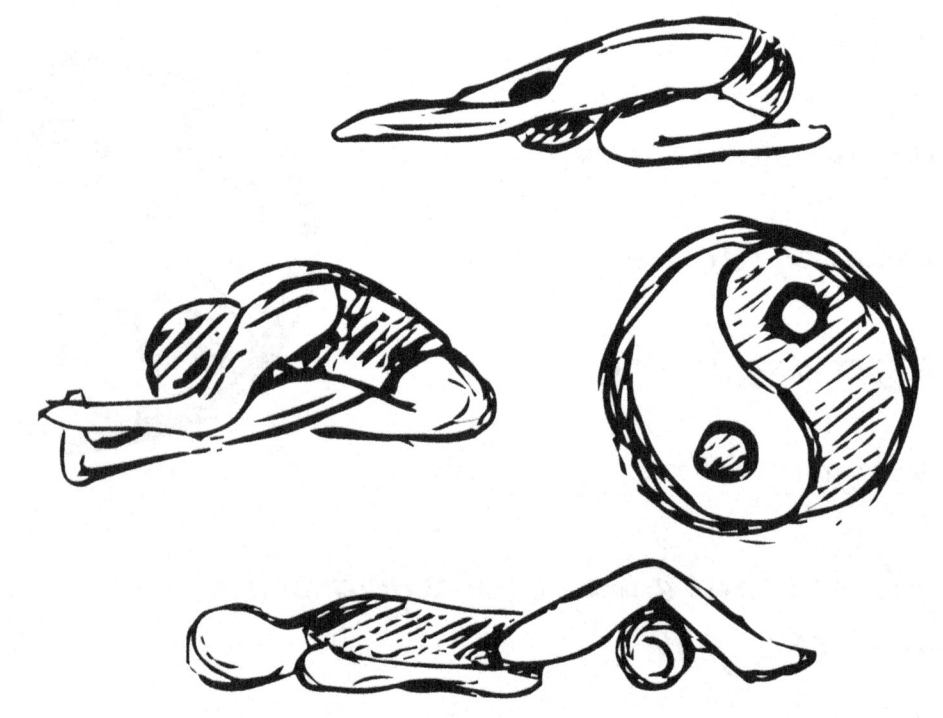

i will catch you if you fall...

yoga mat

Y

Yin Yoga

Reflections

Y

Yin Yoga

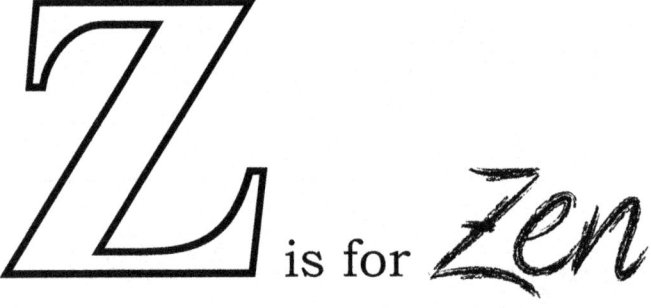

Z is for *Zen*

We have come to the end, Zen! It is appropriate that Z and Zen is our final letter as having a ZEN attitude is an outcome of the behaviors and suggestions shared in this journal. An attitude of Zen can be described as living in the moment, BEING HERE NOW!

Notes about *Zen*:

_____

_____

_____

_____

Z
Zen

 *Write down the first words or phrases that come to mind when describing what "Zen" looks and feels like to you.*

 *How will the suggestions in this journal and your responses support a state of Zen?*

Z
Zen

Ten to Zen

1. Let go of comparing
2. Let go of competing
3. Let go of anger
4. Let go of judgments
5. Let go of worrying
6. Let go of regrets
7. Let go of blame
8. Let go of guilt
9. Let go of fear
10. Let go of perfection

Remember–you can cultivate a life of calm!

Z

Zen

_____

_____

_____

_____

_____

_____

_____

_____

_____

Z
Zen

In Summary

My deepest wish is that you have been inspired by the understanding that you have choice to create and live in ease! By incorporating behaviors that bring ease, and making these behaviors become your habit or way of being, you WILL experience a transformation. Decision making becomes much clearer using the filter of ease: anxiety and stress will be reduced; tough times will be managed with grace and strength; and optimal health and well-being will be experienced physically, mentally, emotionally and spiritually! Why not give yourself the gift of ease?

I recommend that you review this Journal from time to time. You may have something different to say the next time you answer the questions. ☺

Please share with me any new insights, learnings and "ah ha's" to leannelkins@hotmail.com I would love to hear from you! ♡

Namaste,

LeAnn

Follow us on Facebook and Instagram at Chaos to Ease –OR– www.chaostoease.com

A to Z

What is Chaos to Ease to you using your own ABC's?

A is for _____

B is for _____

C is for _____

D is for _____

E is for _____

F is for _____

G is for _____

H is for _____

I is for _____

J is for _____

K is for _____

L is for _____

M is for _____

N is for _____

O is for _____

P is for _____

Q is for _____

R is for _____

S is for _____

T is for _____

U is for _____

V is for _____

W is for _____

X is for _____

Y is for _____

Z is for _____

My Story

"I have no stress in my life!"

LeAnn

I wasn't calling it stress but in conversations with my coach I became aware that the bad attitude, aggressive behavior, judgement of self and others, lack of quiet time, "intense" workouts, constant dieting, and filling my days with non-stop activity was indeed stress. Then there was the internal chaos – my thinking and my thoughts – the ones that said "you are not enough," "you need to be thinner, smarter, stronger, nicer...," "you should do this or you should do that," "you messed up," "why didn't you speak up, you are stupid," "you need to work long hours to show your worth," "you don't deserve...," "you need to be busy all of the time," "show them you can do it all and don't need any help," "don't let anyone see you being anything other than strong and able," "don't be such a baby, just suck it up!" These are just some examples of the thousands of thoughts I had daily which caused internal chaos leading to stressful living.

Let me back up a bit and share some defining moments of my own story that have contributed to choices and behaviors that created and fueled the chaos. Let's start with my teen years. Like many teens I craved being

popular and fitting in. Being shy, striking up conversations and making friends was hard. I did think making cheer or drill team could be a way to join the click of popular girls. Being part of that group is where I thought true happiness, joy and belonging existed. Now while I did try out for both cheer and drill (more than once so "go me" for not giving up!), I do not have any rhythm or dance abilities in my body (still experienced today in any Zumba class you may see me taking!) so it is no surprise that I never made any of those squads. I was devasted though at the time and the feeling of not fitting in remained.

Still seeking a place to belong, I joined flag corp -- you know the group that does coordinated drills with flags as part of band? I loved it! I knew it wasn't the most popular group but I had found a group. There was a lot of joy and happiness in belonging until I overheard some "mean girls" (whom I worshipped – yes, how sad) talking about band and flag corps members being nerds, cracking jokes and making fun of us. So my takeaway (oh to be able to give my 14 year old self a hug and let her know she is worthy just as she is and those mean girls have just as many insecurities and doubts as she does) was it really wasn't cool to be part of flag corp and it was much more important to quit than to be part of a group being made fun of by the popular girls. So, I quit right before the parade season was underway. At the time I remember having mixed emotions of sadness for missing out but also was glad to not be part of the group the cool kids made fun of. My heart aches

for this girl in thinking of the loneliness I was experiencing yet not talking about, as well the decisions I was making to try to be more connected to the popular crowd.

This sense of wanting to be part of the cool group stuck with me throughout high school. I believe this is why when I think of high school I have mostly a negative reaction. The truth is I received an excellent education and excelled academically yet I never publicly shared that I was in honor society and in fact would never talk about honor society meetings (thinking people would think me uncool)! This was also weird because I worked so hard to get good grades and it was important to me yet I didn't want my peers to know. It was all about the "show" and how I wanted the world to see me. This theme would carry on for decades -- the theme of putting forward the face I wanted others to see. This creates such internal strife and stress. So easy to see in retrospect but not visible at all in the moment. Seems asinine now. Yet, as I mentioned, it wasn't a fleeting moment but the beginning of the game face I created for the world to see. I know I'm not alone in this -- many of us do this. The question that came to me much later shook me. At what cost?

These years are also when I thought being thin would help me be part of the group. I joined my first gym (Living Well Lady) at age 14 with the money I earned babysitting. My relationship with working out and fitness was underway. Now while there were definitely benefits to my health, it was also

the start of working out for the wrong reasons. Mainly to overcome any "bad eating," to look a certain way (the right amount of muscle with little fat) and to lose weight. Because losing weight helps you fit in, right? And this is also the time "dieting" became a way of life. From counting calories to skipping meals & eliminating foods — Weight Watchers, Adkins, Cabbage Soup, Whole 30, Paleo, Cleanses and Fasts and that is just to name a few — can anyone else relate? The idea of weighing a particular number, wearing a particular size and being "thin" was such a goal that it not only caused stress but stopped me from enjoying life in many ways. Yes, not eating donuts or chips anytime I wanted did and does promote better health but being obsessed with not eating unhealthy (or what I deemed unhealthy) foods for the sake of appearance and acceptance is not a behavior conducive to happiness and ease. Those behaviors started in my young years and the true beliefs that triggered those behaviors would follow me throughout my life. Truthfully, I still fight them today. But one thing I do know now: being stressed about weight and exercise is not a way to live in ease.

In these teenage years I was searching for, joy, happiness, and belonging while not recognizing that all of that was available inside of me. If only I knew I was enough! When I look at pictures of me from high school I now see a beautiful young lady. Not fat, not ugly, not unworthy. But so hard for me to see that then. These were formative years and experiences which would absolutely impact me as I entered adulthood and my professional life.

Upon graduating from college, I started my employment at The Boeing Company which would last almost two decades. And, with three kids arriving within the first five years of employment, I quickly stepped into the role of "working mother!" "Just be a super woman -- a business professional, mom, wife, friend, volunteer, etc." is what I told myself. There was never a choice not to work. I had my college degree and a good job so of course I would work. It was the start of a love/hate relationship with my career. The message was: you can have it all and do it all with ease! Oh, how far from the truth was that statement.

I will say the years of my kids being little were my most organized. When you have to get three kids under five up and out the door to daycare by 5:30am you'd better be organized. Yet, there was an expense to this organization especially since it isn't my natural way. This was the start of my being a drill sergeant. Things had to get done a certain way at a certain time which led to black and white thinking and not being open to alternatives. While a lot of stuff got done, there was no time taken that resembled slowing down. Who has time to grab a book and read? Visit with friends? Take a yoga class; too slow! You must take a "hard" class! Relax in the bath? Journal or do any kind of introspective work? Certainly not I! At the time I felt I was serving my family, yet over the years I started to realize I was adding another layer of stress, not only to myself: others felt it too!

Professionally speaking I excelled -- I was good at my job as a corporate facilitator and instructional design consultant. In many ways it was my career where I found confidence, my "voice," and felt a real connection in being part of a group. It was also where I observed and learned through experience that for a woman to be respected, listened to, promoted, and valued it was best to not only speak up often but do so in an aggressive, know it all, and maybe even bitchy manner. Now this isn't exclusively true but there are most certainly elements to the truth in this belief I held and acted upon. There were definitely times in my career that I was leading from a place of that drill sergeant and I absolutely demonstrated behaviors to maintain this persona. While it wasn't present 100% of the time, when I was feeling stressed and pressured (which did happen a good amount of the time), that side of me took over. I often knew it was happening but there wasn't much that could be done to stop these behaviors, even momentarily. Or so I thought!

Then my world flipped and I was faced with a major medical crisis. At 36 years old I had a stroke which led to open heart surgery and a long physical recovery. My life, as I knew it, both personally and professionally was put on hold. My mom took over on the home front and wouldn't you know it, work went on just fine without my presence! I was forced to slow down physically (literally could barely walk and it was weeks before I could even attempt a flight of stairs) and internally things were still "chaotic!" I did absolutely

feel blessed to have survived but I was also pissed off to be dealing with the recovery. "Why me?" was an ongoing mantra and there were months of a negative attitude being taken out on those around me (sorry family). My total focus was to get better physically as soon as possible so I could get back to my life -- yes, the drill sergeant one! I had no time for this sitting around, not working, gaining weight, and losing strength by not going to the gym. It would be lovely if I could say that it was during this recovery that I found some inner peace and calm but I did nothing to create the calm. In fact, I didn't even know that "calm and ease" were missing in my life. Once I had my energy back, I quickly got back into my old habits. The old patterns returned and stayed in control for almost 7 more years.

It was during these years that my professional work was the hardest as I joined my new husband in owning a successful consulting company. Long hours, lots and lots of travel, leading a group of consultants, and serving on the leadership team. There were also three teenagers living at home -- now, just having three teens in the house is stressful enough but add to that the pressures with the business and not having any regular practices in my day to day life that would lessen the stress and chaos -- it is amazing I got out of that time in one piece. Or did I?

The end of those seven years gave another opportunity to slow down, or should I say forced me. I was diagnosed with Cancer.

I got the call from the doctor telling me I had cancer while sitting in the back of a cab in New York City on a business trip. It was one of those intense stomach drop, adrenalin rush moments. Believe it or not, one of my first thoughts following the call was "why have I spent so much time daily worrying about what I eat, how much I weigh and spending so much time at the gym?" These thoughts were not about wishing I had just eaten whatever I wanted and not worked out since I was going to get cancer anyway; they were about priorities in my life and wishing that I hadn't spent so much time worrying about things that didn't matter. For a while I made an effort to realign my priorities, but in a short amount of time I fell back into the chaos of business travel and the busyness of life. The cancer diagnosis, while caught early, did mean it was necessary to quickly have a radical hysterectomy. What that basically means is I woke up from surgery, at age 44, in full blown menopause. Not only was I managing the emotions connected with cancer, my hormones were completely whacky and I know I wasn't a joy to be around. This could have been the time that I started really living in ease as explored in this journal, however, I must admit that a cancer diagnosis and surgery didn't do the trick either. Maintaining my role as that drill sergeant who got a lot done (I was even told that some of my team thought I was really scary), restricting my diet (because I am only good enough if "thin enough") and doing intense workouts 5 days a week (think "Boot Camp" because it is a waste of time working out unless it is at a 110% push) returned easily. This was the life I continued to live for another four years.

It was after this time period that I left my full-time job and the responsibilities of co-owning a company. I took a break from the work driven LeAnn for the first time since I was 15. It was nice to sleep in, have time to run errands during the weekdays, set my own schedule and just do whatever I wanted. My inner critic kept getting louder and louder as time went by – the critic who said "you should be working!" I listened to that inner voice and a list of "should's" were developed and acted upon. One of the items was to dive back in to consulting (as a contractor so there was more flexibility) but I really didn't have any passion or energy for the work any longer. Another item was to do some sort of continuing education. This led to becoming a Certified Health Coach. A new challenge for me to be back in school and I leapt in committed to giving it my all and earning A's. While I did learn a lot about the science behind food and nutrition, a big motivation during the certification was about the grades and what I would "do" with the certification. Both the grades and the trying to figure out what to "do" caused me a fair amount of stress and anxiety. It is so easy to look back in retrospect and see that I was missing so many fun and joyful moments because I was focused on a particular outcome and not being in the now. Upon receipt of this certification, I immediately set out to do something with it (because the learning itself would never be enough) and designed a 12-week lifestyle course focused on attitude, nutrition and exercise. Thirteen people signed up for the initial course and I thought a new "career" was underway.

Designing and leading this 12-week lifestyle course was what eventually led me to radically transform my way of being. Moving away from a life of stress and chaos to one of connection and being present (or what I like to refer to as BE HERE NOW) and allowing calm and ease to take root. You are probably thinking it was the course itself that started the transformation but it wasn't. It was the feelings I began to recognize while sharing the course with others that initiated the transformation. While I was imparting wisdom and making a difference in a group of lives, I myself was struggling on the inside. Something felt off (hello INTUITION) and there was a disconnect that I couldn't figure out. Between a good friend gracefully telling me that this disconnected feeling may be because I wasn't really "living and doing the work myself" and my coach guiding me to see I was creating and seeking stress and chaos (after declaring to her "I have no stress in my life!") was I able to grasp what the internal struggle was all about. Decision made. It was time to move past the chaos and find the ease! Or I could say, decision "finally" made. There had been hundreds of missed opportunities along the way although I believe these missed opportunities were all important parts of my journey and I fully appreciate these experiences today!

With the on-going support of my coach, family, friends and my husband, I am indeed living differently and have transformed my life. My life now is one of contentment and happiness, a rebirth of sorts, filled with creativity and energy and being a counselor for self and others. There have been ups

and downs along the way. Things eliminated or significantly reduced like caffeine, rushing around, intense exercise and alcohol. New behaviors added that are now the norm like meditation, down time, self-care, rituals and yoga. A different approach to viewing life that withholds judgment, is filled with joy and gratitude, and is patient and kind. This journal is a culmination of this transformation (a work still and always in progress). While all of the lessons are personal to me, may you have found lessons along the way to support you in living like the lotus – at ease in muddy waters!

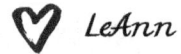 LeAnn

Resources

Some authors whom I have been inspired by and can provide more in depth knowledge on topics covered include:

Shawn Achor

Sarah Ban Breathnach

Gabrielle Bernstein

Brene' Brown

Deepak Chopra

Jae Ellard

Louise Hay

Dali Lama

Glennon Doyle Melton

Anita Moorjani

Rebecca Scritchfield

Eckart Tolle

To my mentor, coach & counselor -- Erin
for your light, love and guidance

To my sister friend --Jae
for your grace, feedback and encouragement

To my brand strategist -- Ashley
for your creative thoughts,
strategic mind and resourcefullness

To my tribe of women
for your inspiration, courage and support

To my best friend & husband -- Craig
for your wisdom, patience and devotion

May you live like the **Lotus**,
at ease in Muddy Waters!

About the Author

In addition to her quest of living the work suggested in this journal, she enjoys spending time with friends and family (including 3 grandchildren) and traveling with her husband. For more in-depth information, please read My Story starting on page 116.

Made in the USA
Monee, IL
12 December 2019